THIS BEAUTIFUL CITY

CREATED BY **THE CIVILIANS**
WRITTEN BY **STEVEN COSSON**
AND **JIM LEWIS**

MUSIC AND LYRICS BY
MICHAEL FRIEDMAN

FROM INTERVIEWS BY
EMILY ACKERMAN, MARSHA STEPHANIE BLAKE,
BRAD HEBERLEE, STEPHEN PLUNKETT,
ALISON WELLER, AND THE AUTHORS

DRAMATISTS
PLAY SERVICE
INC.

THIS BEAUTIFUL CITY
Copyright © 2010, Steven Cosson, Jim Lewis, Michael Friedman

All Rights Reserved

SPECIAL NOTE

Anyone receiving permission to produce THIS BEAUTIFUL CITY is required to give credit to the Authors as sole and exclusive Authors of the Play on the title page of all programs distributed in connection with performances of the Play and in all instances in which the title of the Play appears for purposes of advertising, publicizing or otherwise exploiting the Play and/or a production thereof. The names of the Authors must appear on a separate line, in which no other names appear, immediately beneath the title and in size of type equal to 50% of the size of the largest, most prominent letter used for the title of the Play. No person, firm or entity may receive credit larger or more prominent than that accorded the Authors. The billing must appear as follows:

2

THIS BEAUTIFUL CITY
Created by The Civilians
Written by Steven Cosson and Jim Lewis
Music and Lyrics by Michael Friedman

The following acknowledgments must appear on the title page in all programs distributed in connection with performances of the Play:

THIS BEAUTIFUL CITY was developed from interviews conducted by
Emily Ackerman, Marsha Stephanie Blake, Brad Heberlee,
Stephen Plunkett, Alison Weller, and the authors.

Commissioned and developed by The Civilians
(Steven Cosson, Artistic Director; Marion Friedman, Managing Director)
with the assistance of the Sundance Institute, Colorado College,
and Center Theatre Group.

Development supported in part by the National Endowment for the Arts
and Z-Space Studio, San Francisco, CA.

World Premiere co-produced by
the 2008 Humana Festival of New American Plays
at Actors Theatre of Louisville
and by the Studio Theatre in Washington, DC
as part of its 2008 Opening Our Doors Initiative.

THIS BEAUTIFUL CITY was co-produced by
Center Theatre Group, LA, 2008 and Vineyard Theatre, NY, 2009.

ACKNOWLEDGMENTS

Dramaturg:
Jocelyn Clarke

Research Dramaturgs:
Jana Goold, Abigail Katz, Donya Washington

Associate Research Dramaturgs:
Ari Agbabian, Li Cornfeld, Zac Kline, Michele Travis

Producing Director:
Kyle Gordon

Associate Producer:
Jess Chayes

THIS BEAUTIFUL CITY was developed in a residency January 8th–February 14th, 2007 at Colorado College, Tom Lindblade, Drama and Dance Department Chair, with students Chris Benz, Katherine E. Dawson, Ellen J. Evers, Christine Gonzalez, Vincent Gumlich, Alexandra Hesbrook, Robin Hutchins, Hugh Johnson, Elizabeth Kancilia, Annie Kelvie, Sarah Lee, Meghan Murrah, and Adam Stone

The Civilians is deeply grateful to the people of Colorado Springs who participated in the creation of this play. While it is impossible to list all the individuals and organizations who participated in this project, The Civilians thanks those organizations that offered significant and ongoing support: New Life Church, The Mill, the Revolution House of Prayer, Vanguard Church, The Citizens Project, Emmanuel Baptist Church, Woodmen Valley Chapel, and Coloradans for Fairness and Equality.

AUTHORS' NOTE

THIS BEAUTIFUL CITY was created based on extensive interviews with numerous residents of Colorado Springs. Some of the characters are based entirely on one individual; others are fictional creations inspired by several different interviews. The play can be performed with six or more actors. While other combinations are possible, The Civilians' production used three men and three women in the following breakdown:

> **WOMAN 1:** Atheist Activist, Young Woman — God's Grace, T-girl Christian, others.

> **WOMAN 2:** Economic Development Woman, Fairness Leader, RHOP Member, "End Times" singer, others.

> **WOMAN 3:** Converted Woman, "Whatever" singer, Emmanuel Choir Member, Ben Reynolds, New Pastor at Emmanuel, Air Force Cadet, others.

> **MAN 1:** Associate Pastor, Fairness Worker, Ted Emails singer, Reporter, Air Force Cadet, others.

> **MAN 2:** Alt Writer, Mikey Weinstein, RHOP Leader, others.

> **MAN 3:** TAG Pastor, Priest, Air Force Cadet, Ted Haggard, Marcus Haggard, others.

NOTE FROM COMPOSER/LYRICIST

THIS BEAUTIFUL CITY was performed in Los Angeles and New York with a four-piece band (keyboard/guitar doubling, bass, drums, guitar/mandolin/banjo doubling) and with one of the actors on stage playing guitar in the New Life Church scenes. A simpler version can be performed without the doublings in the band (just keyboard and guitar) and even without the onstage guitar, though the actor playing guitar helps define the atmosphere of New Life.

THIS BEAUTIFUL CITY received its world premiere at the Actors Theatre of Louisville Humana Festival of New American Plays in Louisville, Kentucky, in a co-production with Studio Theatre, opening on March 5, 2008. It was directed by Steven Cosson; the choreography was by Chase Brock; the set design and projections were by Debra Booth; the costume design was by Lorraine Venberg; the lighting design was by Deb Sullivan; the sound design was by Matt Callahan; and the music direction was by Scott Anthony. The cast was as follows: Emily Ackerman, Marsha Stephanie Blake, Ian Brennan, Brad Heberlee, Dori Legg, and Stephen Plunkett. The musicians were as follows: Anthony Gantt and Ben Short.

THIS BEAUTIFUL CITY was subsequently presented at Studio Theatre in Washington, D.C., in a co-production with the Actors Theatre of Louisville, opening on June 11, 2008. It was directed by Steven Cosson; the musical staging was by Chase Brock; the set design and projections were by Debra Booth; the costume design was by Lorraine Venberg; the lighting design was by Michael Giannitti; the sound design was by Erik Trester; and the music direction was by Gabriel Mangiante. The cast was as follows: Emily Ackerman, Marsha Stephanie Blake, Aysan Çelik, Matthew Dellapina, Brad Heberlee, and Stephen Plunkett. The musicians were as follows: Anders Eliasson and Robin Rhodes.

THIS BEAUTIFUL CITY was produced by Center Theatre Group, at the Kirk Douglas Theatre in Los Angeles, California, in a co-production with Vineyard Theatre, opening on September 21, 2008. It was directed by Steven Cosson; the choreography was by John Carrafa; the set design was by Neil Patel; the costume design was by Alix Hester; the lighting design was by David Weiner; the sound design was by Ken Travis; the projections were by Jason H. Thompson; and the music direction was by Erik James. The cast was as follows: Emily Ackerman, Marsha Stephanie Blake, Brad Heberlee, Brandon Miller, Stephen Plunkett, and Alison Weller. The musicians were as follows: Tom Corbett, Mike Schadel, and Brian Duke Song.

THIS BEAUTIFUL CITY was produced by Vineyard Theatre in New York, in a co-production with Center Theatre Group, opening on February 22, 2009. It was directed by Steven Cosson; the choreography was by John Carrafa; the set design was by Neil Patel; the costume design was by Alix Hester; the lighting design was by David Weiner; the sound design was by Ken Travis; the projections were by Jason H. Thompson; and the music direction was by Erik James. The cast was as follows: Emily Ackerman, Marsha Stephanie Blake, Brad Heberlee, Brandon Miller, Stephen Plunkett, and Alison Weller. The musicians were as follows: Chris Biesterfeldt, Benjamin Campbell, and Richard Huntley.

CHARACTERS
(in order of appearance)

ECONOMIC DEVELOPMENT WOMAN

CONVERTED WOMAN

ASSOCIATE PASTOR

ATHEIST ACTIVIST

ALT WRITER

TAG PASTOR

YOUNG WOMAN — GOD'S GRACE

FAIRNESS WORKER

FAIRNESS LEADER

PRIEST

EMMANUEL CHOIR MEMBER

T-GIRL CHRISTIAN

TED HAGGARD

TRAILS GUIDES

AIR FORCE ACADEMY CADETS

MIKEY WEINSTEIN

RHOP MEMBERS

RHOP LEADER

ONLINE CHAT POSTERS

REPORTER

BEN REYNOLDS

MARCUS HAGGARD

NEW PASTOR AT EMMANUEL

PLACE

Colorado Springs, Colorado.

TIME

Leading up to, and after, the 2006 election.

Work for the well-being of the city where I have sent you,
and pray to the Lord for this. For if it is well with the city you
live in, it will be well with you.

—JEREMIAH 29:7 (NLV)

THIS BEAUTIFUL CITY

Scene 1

Cowboys

A member of the company enters and speaks to the audience.

ECONOMIC DEVELOPMENT WOMAN. Let me make sure I understand this. OK. Well, my assistant came in today and asked to run something *really* outside the box by me. She told me there's this theater company from New York looking to write a play from real interviews with real people about the evangelical Christians in Colorado Springs and she asked if I would be willing to have a meeting. And I sat there saying, are you kidding me? But OK, go ahead. *(Question.)* Well, what happened was, twenty-two years ago my husband lost his job in Detroit, and I got a job offer to come to Colorado Springs to do economic development. My background was business attraction. But moving to a different city is a big, big, step. It's scary. So I found a verse, Proverbs 16:3, uhh … and it goes something like, I know the plans I have for you, plans for the future, not plans for disaster, and I took that to mean that it was His plan I come. So I did. I drove out here with tears rolling down my face the whole way. Then when I got here I thought wow, this is a gorgeous city. It would be a wonderful place to sell. So that's what I did. And ultimately, what I personally recruited was fifteen Christian non-profit organizations, some of them were two- and three-employee companies and now, well, at least four of these organizations have revenues of over one hundred million dollars.

And, and, I didn't intend or let's see, I didn't even think about ummmm … I was just doing what I could do well with the contacts that I had. And if God was using me to make this city the evangelical capitol, I didn't know it at the time.

So, can I ask you a pretty forward question? OK, um. Is there a particular slant that you would like to put on…? The reason I ask is because people have their ideas: "right-wing fundamental evangelical" and I want to say to people if your whole belief of who we are is formed through the media, then let me buy you lunch. *(Music starts.)* Come spend some time here and you'll see a lot of people and a lot of families in this city leading better lives, and then we can talk. *(The rest of the company has entered. Three of them sing as the Colorado Wranglers, a cowboy trio. Song: Colorado.)*

COLORADO WRANGLERS.
    IT'S A LONG ROAD TO COLORADO
    WALKING 'NEATH THAT ROCKY MOUNTAIN MOON
    WHETHER HONEST MAN OR DESPERADO
    YOU WILL FIND A NEW LIFE SOON

CONVERTED WOMAN. So my story: I had this drug deal that went bad and had to get out of town, and I wound up in Colorado Springs, because I had this really good childhood friend here. Only, she was so different. She was married and had a family. And they were clean and straight and conservative-looking. And she used to be an acid freak back in the day. But she and her husband were the first people I encountered that were really living what they said they believed. So I went to church with her and that was the first time I ever really prayed. I was all by myself. And I said, "God, if you're real, prove it." *(Music stops.)* And someone put his hand on my shoulder and said, "Just believe I'm real." *(Music starts.)* The room was empty. But it was a hand. I felt it. Freaked me out. I kept a diary at the time and it said, "I need to get out of Colorado before Jesus gets me!" So I got on a bus and went to San Francisco. Because Jesus couldn't possibly be in San Francisco. But eventually I came back here, and I told my friend I wanted to get saved. I didn't want to go down to the altar. I was still a little *(Gesture meaning uncomfortable.)* So she got two friends and we went to Baskin-Robbins, ordered ice cream and stood in a circle and prayed. And I asked Jesus Christ to come into my life. *(Pause.)* And then we ate ice cream.

COLORADO WRANGLERS.
    HOW COULD WE CHANGE OUR MOTTO
    HOW COULD WE CHANGE OUR TUNE
    IT'S A LONG ROAD TO COLORADO
    BUT WE WILL BE THERE SOON

ASSOCIATE PASTOR. For me, it was my junior year of high school. I had a very rocky relationship with an alcoholic father, and I was taking after him. But my little sister was a very active member of New Life, and she started encouraging me to go. Look — you go to the services and people were jumping around, it's kooky, but it was just this truly joyful and liberating experience. So I kept coming. I never really had a positive male influence in my life, but Ted Haggard taught me that I could be exceptional, that I could serve other people and think of them first instead of myself. And now that I'm one of the Associate Pastors here at New Life, now I've got people looking to me for guidance.

COLORADO WRANGLERS.

    AND THE WORLD WILL LOOK TO COLORADO
    WHEN WE BUILD THAT CITY ON A HILL
    IT WILL BE A CHRISTIAN EL DORADO
    AN EXAMPLE OF GOD'S WILL

ATHEIST ACTIVIST. Well I've pretty much lived here all my life. *(She stops the music with a gesture.)* We're atheists and my business is Evolve Fish. You know, the little Darwin fish that have legs? *(Music starts back up.)* We've got a shop and we do mail order. And when we first started, we would get death threats, phone calls at two in the morning. When we bought our house we chose a high elevation so people just couldn't come up and we thought about where the windows are. I'm OK with it. I'm up for the fight. But it's hard on our daughter. She's seven. And she's afraid that if her friends find out we don't believe that they won't be her friends anymore. *(Music speeds up.)* And what do I tell her?

Colorado Springs was always a conservative military town but back in the eighties it got more and more religious. And there is a *big* difference! But you know they've seeded the military here with born-agains. Like with the cadets at the Air Force Academy. You know, if someone wants to be an off-the-edge snake handler, I don't care! *(Music gets louder.)* But when they endanger my life, or the lives of my children and my country because they let this insanity take hold, then I'm scared!

COLORADO WRANGLERS.

    KEEP SINGIN' WITH BRAVADO
    FILL THE MOUNTAINS WITH THIS TUNE
    IT'S A LONG ROAD TO COLORADO
    BUT WE WILL BE THERE SOON

COLORADO WRANGLER. We're the Colorado Wranglers. We used to be a five-piece cowboy band and we worked at the Flying W Chuckwagon Diner. But then — you know we're Christians, right? We got the call from God, and we had to leave there, so now there are three of us. I'm not blaming anybody, but as we got older and older we got bolder and bolder in our faith. The Flying W is a secular place, and we started pushing the envelope and talking about the Lord, and the people there started saying, y'all are doin' too much, and they told us to pray about it. And we prayed about it, and God told us to leave. It wasn't a hard decision; when God tells you to do something, you do it.

TAG PASTOR. I came here from Washington right after college, and well …
(Sings.)
> IN COLLEGE I PARTIED ALL OF THE TIME.
> GIRLS GIRLS JUST CONSTANTLY THINKING LOTSA MONEY, A
>   NICE HOUSE
> I USED TO WANT A BIG BIG BOAT.
> EVERYTHING WAS GREAT.
> EXCEPT I STARTED THINKING ABOUT DEATH
> YOU KNOW YOU LIVE FOR SIXTY, SEVENTY YEARS
> MAYBE EIGHTY, NINETY IF YOU'RE LUCKY
> AND THEN WHAT?
> WHAT WAS IT FOR?
> MAKING LOTS OF MONEY
> GETTING A NICE HOUSE?
> AND A BIG BIG BOAT?
> I WAS LYING IN BED ONE MORNING WITH MY GIRLFRIEND.
> SHE WAS HOT.
> WE'D BEEN TOGETHER FOR A WHILE AND WE WERE AT THE
>   PLACE OF, YOU KNOW, ARE WE GONNA GET SERIOUS
> SHE WANTED TO GET MARRIED.
> AND SHE TURNED TO ME AND SAID,
> IS THIS GOING ANYWHERE
> AND I FELT GOD PULLING ON MY HEART.
> AND I SAID NO. NO
> AND I LEFT
> MAN, SHE WAS GORGEOUS.
> WHAT WAS I THINKING?!
> THEN I STOPPED DRINKING

GROUP A.
> WHEN WE BUILD THIS WORLD IN COLORADO
> YOU WILL HEAR THAT VOICE FROM UP ABOVE
> EVERY FELIX, FRIDA, FRITZ, AND OTTO
> SOON WILL FEEL GOD'S HEALING LOVE
>
> LIVE LIKE YOU'VE WON THE LOTTO
> WHEREVER YOU MAY ROAM
> IT'S A LONG ROAD TO COLORADO
> 'TIL YOU HAVE REACHED YOUR HOME

TAG PASTOR. *(Simultaneous.)*
AND I WENT HOME AND I STARTED TO PRAY.
I CLOSED MY EYES AND I STARTED TO SAY.
GOD IF YOU ARE THERE YOU KNOW SAY SOMETHING
PLEASE SAY SOMETHING.
AND FOR A MOMENT I FELT NOT A THING.
BUT THEN I HEARD IT, THE VOICE OF THE LORD.
I FOUND THE ANSWER
IF YOU LEARN TO LISTEN GOD WILL SPEAK TO YOU.
I LIVE THE WAY I LIVE BECAUSE I
I WANT TO BE CLOSE TO MY GOD AND
I AM A CHRISTIAN BECAUSE I LOVE GOD.
I LOVE TO SPEND EVERY MINUTE WITH HIM.
I LOVE TO SPEND TIME ALONE WITH HIM.
I DON'T NEED MONEY, SUCCESS, OR A BIG BOAT
OR A BIG BOAT. YOU KNOW?

Scene 2

Two Coffeeshops

Projection: "A Trails Guide to Pikes Peak Country."

VOICEOVER. A Trails Guide to Pikes Peak Country.

TRAILS GUIDE #1. This comprehensive guide is designed to answer all your questions, and more. So to get the most out of your time here in the beautiful Colorado Rockies, use this guide as you would use a walking, talking human one to help you discover the secret wonders of the land that only the locals know. Also, use this book to ensure a safe journey. Because there are some real dangers in the mountains — though not always the ones you might imagine. *(Associate Pastor in a coffee shop at New Life Church.)*

ASSOCIATE PASTOR. Did you have a hard time finding the coffee shop? No, this is New Life's World Prayer Center. Next door is the main worship center, and the building past that is the theater which is mostly used by the twenty-something ministry. *(Question.)* Well sure I guess New Life is a megachurch. But it doesn't feel big. It feels like you know everybody. So what are you guys doing, exactly? Huh. No, that doesn't sound too weird. Seriously, at New Life we've got an open door policy. That's always been a big thing for Pastor Ted. So what do you want to know? *(Question.)* Well New Life started about twenty-five years ago. Yeah well when Ted Haggard first came to Colorado, he went on a prayer fasting retreat. Just to spend some time alone with God up in the mountains. He pitched his tent and prayed and fasted. And God gave him a vision for a church, a big church impacting the community. So then Ted and Gayle started New Life in their basement. Then it moved to a Holiday Inn or something, and then over the years more and more evangelicals were moving to the Springs and New Life kept growing and now it's yeah, the congregation is fourteen thousand. It's pretty amazing being a part of that. *(Alt Writer at a different coffee shop in downtown Colorado Springs.)*

ALT WRITER. It was like a zombie movie or something. To me. Right after I went to college, the evangelicals just sorta invaded. Though you wouldn't necessarily notice it here in downtown. The Christians tend to live out there in the sprawl. Yeah, isn't this place great? Thank god there's still a few places that aren't a Starbucks or a Borders. So what do you want to know? Well, I grew up in Colorado Springs. I left, but then my wife and I moved back with our son to be near my mom. And my stepdad, who's my dad's lover. No, my dad's dead. And my mom's a lesbian. Yeah. *Yeah. (Laughs.)*

So, I came home in 2001 and around that time New Life was getting huge — Ted Haggard — and, you know, they built that monstrosity of a building out there. *(Clarifying.)* In the north. *(Pointing.)* This way. No, that's … Look, let me help you, it's easy. You've got the Rockies and Pikes Peak in the west, right, so that'll always be there to orient you, you'll see them wherever you are. And then in the northeast in the middle of nothing, there's New Life and Focus on the Family — Focus on the Family? James Dobson? It's like the biggest conservative Christian media empire in the world. Yeah. Did you like, read anything before you came here? OK, so also up north on the other side of the highway you've got the Air Force Academy. And south is Fort Carson. Ent Air Force Base is due east and inside the mountain is NORAD. Yeah, War Games. Totally. And in between is Manitou Springs, all new-agey crystals and dreamcatchers and shit, and downtown you've got the hippy kids at Colorado College and all the rest of us. Yeah, to the Christians downtown is like Satan's personal den of iniquity.

ASSOCIATE PASTOR. So yeah, as New Life was growing, Pastor Ted really encouraged the church to look outward to the whole city. He put the idea of city transformation into the church's DNA. City transformation? Well you should read Ted's book, *Loving Your City into the Kingdom.* But the short version is …

it's about turning things around in a troubled city using strategic prayer. Just using the power of prayer you can see measurable outcomes like better jobs, fewer divorces, less crime. Yeah.

ALT WRITER. The way my mom tells it, before all the evangelicals moved in, Colorado Springs was very live and let live. But what happened was: in the eighties this city brought in evangelical non-profits to jumpstart the economy. Yeah! Then New Life exploded, Focus on the Family relocated here, Amendment Two happened, which banned any kind of gay rights. This is back in 1992. Colorado got boycotted. And that was it. Colorado was the Hate State and we were Jesus Springs. It was like, I'm from here?

ASSOCIATE PASTOR. So city transformation was a big thing for Ted and New Life in the nineties, and it's not like the work's done by any means; it's more like the bar's been raised. Part of it is that I think people have finally gotten over some of the scandals of the past like Jimmy Swaggart and Jim Bakker so now they're more receptive to the message, you know, they're willing to trust again. Have you gone to a service yet? You haven't? Well you should go see Ted preach on Sunday, but let's see, tonight's Wednesday so that's TAG, the youth ministry. *(Question.)* Yeah, go. You'll blend right in.

Scene 3

TAG

TAG at New Life Church. New Life band and singers perform as part of the service. Song: This Beautiful City.

NEW LIFE BAND AND SINGERS.
    WE ARE DESPERATE FOR YOU
    WE ARE HUNGRY FOR YOU
    WE ARE EMPTY WITHOUT YOU
    HERE IN THE MIDDLE OF NOWHERE

    WILL YOU FILL US WITH YOUR LOVE
    WILL YOU SHOW US YOUR PLAN
    WILL YOU SHOW US THE WAY TO MAKE YOUR BEAUTIFUL CITY

WHERE ARE WE GOING
HOW DO WE GET THERE
WHAT IS YOUR PLAN FOR THIS
THIS THIS BEAUTIFUL CITY

WHERE ARE WE GOING
HOW DO WE GET THERE
WHAT IS YOUR PLAN FOR THIS
THIS THIS BEAUTIFUL CITY

(The TAG Pastor speaks to a large audience of teenagers.)

TAG PASTOR. You guys, you guys here at TAG, you're the next generation for New Life Church. But what have we become? A country club. You come here and you dance and you sing and you rock out and you see your friends, but where is God in that? Where is prayer? So we're going to change the formula of youth ministry. You know, the great band and the catchy tunes, the bright lights and the cool technical effects, the funny preacher who contorts his body. But see, the church needs to be a place where people make a choice. And you need to make a choice about God. How many people here tonight are ready and willing to make that choice? Just, I promise I won't make you feel weird or uncomfortable. Well, maybe. But raise your hands, raise them up in the air, how many out there? *(He proceeds to call out each person with a hand raised.)* OK, I see one over there one over there raise your hands up high … OK, leaders I just … I just want you to pray with them. *(To audience.)* You know what I need from TAG right now? I need you guys to resolve to love Jesus and show him that you know in your heart why he was crucified. Can you do that? And we're gonna make it so that if you have to say no you have to say no to my face. Or your group leader's face. Your group leader is gonna be the romance to your groove. Now, if you're a visitor tonight you're probably thinking "What in the world did I get myself into? I gotta get outta here." But we're not gonna force you. This is not about force. Come to Christ with me tonight. Let me take you on an awesome journey. Let's walk this walk together. Everybody, everybody in the room, ask Jesus to come to you. Come to me Jesus. Pour into me. Fill me with your awesome love. I want to be your disciple. I want to worship you and praise you and be loved by you. Everybody say yes. Yes! Yes! Yes! Yes! Come to us, Lord. We need you. We need you. Say cleanse me, Lord! Do something new in me! *(Music swells, the kids in the imagined audience are getting saved.)* Stay with me, now. Stay with me. We're gonna end on time today, don't worry. Just everyone be silent. Everybody be silent for a moment and get to know God. *(Silence.)*

Scene 4

A Beautiful Place

ASSOCIATE PASTOR. So what did you think? Did it freak you out? It can be pretty intense for a first-time visitor. *(Question.)* Well, yeah, the conversion experience is a big part of being an evangelical. *(Question.)* What's an evangelical? Well, the definition Pastor Ted uses for the media is that an evangelical is someone who believes that Jesus was the son of God, the Bible is the inerrant word of God, and we must be born again. *(Question.)* Which means … well, it's not about finding out who you are. It's about finding who he is and what he wants for your life. I mean, we're all born as selfish creatures. Being born again means you let that part of your life die so that you can really live. *(Question.)* Yeah, right, that's the "new life."

ALT WRITER. But this is a beautiful place. The mountains. It's beautiful. Did you know Katharine Lee Bates wrote the words to "America the Beautiful" here? From the top of Pike's Peak looking back on the Great Plains. Yeah, she did. This town could have been like Santa Fe. And now it's like I'm living in Middle Earth or something. Like everyone here's always sort of "Mordor is over there and we're all just outside the gates living in the shadows of Mordor." You know? I guess my point is that I think so much of the power of the evangelicals is imaginary. But we *give them* their power 'cause people are afraid. You know, like the local printers here will refuse to print something if they think it'll offend Focus on the Family. 'Cause Focus will find out and cancel their orders. And that's a lot of money. So yeah, Dobson and their ilk — they're bullies. But it only works if people allow themselves to be bullied. People just roll over and bam! They give up their freedom. Here, you want to see something. I started a newspaper called *The Toilet Paper*. And the first feature we did was this thing called "The Church Kicker." So we would just pick a church and go and kick it, and then write a caption about why we kicked it. Take a look: *(Alt Writer shows "Church Kicker" pictures as projections and performs the captions.)* "These are just a just a few of the butt-ugly, strip-mall/warehouse/former-movie-theater variety of churches that litter Colorado Springs and deserve to be kicked." *(Projection.)* "St. Mary's Church gets a kick for saying political candidates are accountable for their positions on gay rights or a woman's right to choose, but that war is not a moral issue." *(Projection.)* "These little ninjas are giving a furious kick to the seventeen-million-dollar-Super-Walmart-sized New Life Church. They think Pastor Ted Haggard is on a crusade to erode the separation of church and state when he should be focused on being a compassionate Christian." Hey, do you want a Church Kicker T-shirt?

ASSOCIATE PASTOR. You know, it's funny to me how liberals are so quick to size up Christians as bigoted and hateful, when really that's what I hear so much from them. It doesn't strike me as very tolerant to bash someone else's beliefs.

ALT WRITER. Look I'm not talking about their beliefs per se. But I think they would agree their beliefs are absolute. Well, absolute belief is stupid where matters of civil law are concerned. Our society is governed by the Constitution, not the Bible. So I think that absolute beliefs should be reserved for spiritual matters and not be imposed on those who don't share those beliefs.

ASSOCIATE PASTOR. Well I think most Christians would agree with that. I know I do. But the first amendment gives me just as much right to publicly express my views. And when it comes to politics, I think every citizen should be involved in the political system. Are liberals saying we shouldn't be involved because we're Christian or really is it because they don't agree with us?

ALT WRITER. OK, bottom line, you don't believe in evolution? Then don't be a scientist. You don't believe in abortion? Don't get one. You don't believe in homosexuality? Don't do it. You want to restrict the rights of other people in this city? FUCK YOU.

Scene 5

Whatever

Song: Whatever.

TEENAGE GIRL.
    I'M NOT RELIGIOUS,
    I MEAN, I'M NOT A CHRISTIAN,
    BUT I DON'T REALLY KNOW IF
    I'M A FREETHINKER,
    I MEAN, I GUESS NOT,
    BUT I'M NOT AN ATHEIST,

OR ANYTHING ELSE,
SO I GUESS …
EVANGELICAL, WAIT … DOES THAT MEAN LIKE CHRISTIAN?
AND LIKE A LOT OF PEOPLE
DON'T KNOW I'M NOT LIKE CHRISTIAN,
LIKE MY BEST FRIENDS KNOW,
BUT MY CHRISTIAN FRIENDS DON'T KNOW
I JUST DON'T KNOW, YOU KNOW?
I JUST DON'T KNOW

I JUST, TRY TO BE FRIENDS WITH PEOPLE WHO WOULDN'T
    JUDGE ME FOR BEING LIKE,
NOT CHRISTIAN, YOU KNOW,
BUT IT'S NOT LIKE I, YA KNOW, GO AROUND SAYING
"OH I'M NOT CHRISTIAN" 'CAUSE THAT WOULD BE LIKE, YOU
    KNOW, WHATEVER
NEW LIFE CHURCH HAS TOTALLY SUCKED IN THE YOUTH OF
    COLORADO SPRINGS 'CAUSE LIKE THE LIGHTS AND THE
    BAND AND THEY'VE GOT FREE STARBUCKS, AND IT'S NOT
    LIKE GOING TO CHURCH, YOU KNOW.
IT'S LIKE GOING TO A CONCERT
LIKE I'LL BE THERE AND BE LIKE,
MAN, THE GUYS IN THE BAND ARE HOT,
THE MUSIC'S AWESOME,
AND SOMETIMES I EVEN FIND MYSELF SINGING ALONG,
AND THEN I THINK ABOUT THE WORDS,
AND IT'S JUST AWKWARD,
I MEAN, WHATEVER.
I MEAN, WHATEVER

LIKE WITH MY FRIENDS ABBY AND SARAH,
LIKE ME AND SARAH USED TO PRETEND THAT WE WERE
    CHRISTIAN
'CAUSE ABBY WAS REALLY LIKE RELIGIOUS,
SO WE USED TO PRETEND, THAT WE WERE, TOO
BUT ONE DAY SARAH LIKE STOPPED GOING TO CHURCH
AND ABBY JUST ABANDONED HER
AND SARAH LIKE FELL INTO THE WRONG CROWD AND NOW
    SHE'S PREGNANT AND THE DAD'S LIKE IN JAIL AND ABBY'S

LIKE, "SEE, THAT'S WHAT HAPPENED 'CAUSE SHE STOPPED FOLLOWING JESUS"

I MEAN, YOU JUST DON'T LIKE FIT IN WITH CERTAIN PEOPLE WHEN YOU'RE OPENLY NOT CHRISTIAN.

BUT LIKE, WHATEVER
BUT LIKE, WHATEVER
BUT LIKE, WHATEVER
BUT LIKE, WHATEVER

Scene 6

Fairness and Equality

Outside in a park/playground we meet a member of New Life, a young woman, with her small kids nearby.

YOUNG WOMAN — GOD'S GRACE. Thanks for meeting me here. I just had to get the kids out of the house. What? (*Looking over at kids at playground.*) Oh, they're fine. OK, so I wanted to start the group at New Life because I felt that Christians in general have like this real nasty view towards homosexuality. I called my group "God's Grace and Homosexuality." Anyhow, I think it is important to have a forum where we could come together and discuss our love of these people, but also not compromise our values. I just wanted to talk about it, you know? I mean there's got to be some middle ground between saying "Oh, everything you do is fine with me" and "You're a sinner and you're going to Hell." Yeah. I was kind of shocked that only two people showed up — I don't know. I felt like people were afraid to come. But who nowadays doesn't have someone in their life who's gay? My father is gay. He just celebrated his ten-year anniversary of his union. Yeah. (*Question.*) For a long time my dad didn't respect our boundaries — you know, "Please! Don't make out with your boyfriend on the couch in front of my children! It's not OK! I don't want to have that talk with them just yet!" Yeah, he thought that because he was in love, and after all, God is love, then we should just respect it. You know? (*Looking at kids.*) Oh, guys! *Behave,* OK? Excuse me.

22

(Staff from Coloradans for Fairness and Equality are walking down the tree-lined sidewalks of a residential neighborhood. They ring a doorbell and a door opens.)

FAIRNESS WORKER. Hi, we're walking around your neighborhood today handing out information about Referendum I. It extends equal state rights to same-sex couples as those that are afforded to married couples. OK.

FAIRNESS LEADER. Would you like to take a flyer? Great. Thanks. *(Door closes.)* Can we talk in between houses, is that OK? OK, so there is a LOT going on here with the mid-term elections, and I don't know what it's like in New York, but here, along with voting for congress, etc. there are a lot of other initiatives on the ballot. And this year there are actually *two* ballot initiatives dealing with same-sex couples. Our campaign, Referendum I, would make it law that same-sex couples could have the same basic rights as married couples. And I'm in charge of the Colorado Springs campaign. Now, the other initiative, Amendment 43, that one would ban gay marriage in the state constitution. And of course that campaign has the support of New Life and Focus on the Family. Have you tried to talk to anyone at Focus? *(Laughs.)* Yeah, I didn't think they'd let you into the Death Star. Are you confused? Referendum I: good for the gays. Amendment 43: bad for the gays. Does that make — ? You got it? OK. Good. *(Laughs. Priest enters. He is in his church's office.)*

PRIEST. What we are trying to do is prevent them from DESTROYING the identity of marriage. Because once you change what marriage fundamentally is, you have destroyed it. So with this marriage amendment, we Catholics got together with the evangelicals. And I'll hear criticism of why are you getting involved in politics — well let me tell you something *there is no separation of church and state.* The First Amendment prohibits the government from establishing a state religion, that's quite different. If you look for the phrase "separation of church and state" you will not find those words in the constitution. It's in some letters that Madison wrote but it is *not* in the constitution.

FAIRNESS WORKER. And this marriage amendment thing is happening on the federal level, too. Yeah, they're trying to put it in the U.S. Constitution. Ted Haggard's campaigning for that one, too. You know Ted's president of the National Association of Evangelicals, which represents like, whatever, thirty million people? So Ted talks to the White House once a week. Yeah, the president calls *him.*

FAIRNESS LEADER. It's funny, with this job friends of mine from out of town will ask me, "Well you're not gay, why do you care?" Because that's how we think, right? We each care about our own issues. Well the Christian right, they don't think like that. And I'm not necessarily talking about all the goobers who go to New Life; I'm talking about their *politicized* leaders, 'kay? They've got a big picture and it has to do with big things like dismantling social programs and priva-

tizing public education 'cause the more they can dismantle, the more people need the church to provide those services. Those "Faith-Based Initiatives," that's billions of taxpayer dollars. And what do you think that means for the Christian leaders? Power and money. It's about power and money. And this gay marriage panic is just a means to an end for them. *(To Worker.)* Do you want to do this one?
FAIRNESS WORKER. Sure. *(Rings bell.)* Hi, we're handing out some information about Referendum I, it's not gay marriage — *(Back to the church office.)*
PRIEST. It's gay marriage is what it is. And they don't say that and that's the stealth of it. It's the camel getting his nose under the tent. God started with marriage. It is the most sacred foundation of life. It's how he created the world and the ARROGANCE of those who would try to change that! That is government pretending to play God. They'll argue it's about rights but it's not, it's *temptation.* You see, evil has no power. Remember *Star Wars?* The Emperor had no power. It's only through Darth Vader. In the Garden of Eden the snake had no power, so all he can do is tempt Eve to eat of the tree. Abortion, stem-cell research, gay marriage, all that stuff is ultimately no different than in the Garden of Eden *(Whispering.)* "Eat the fruit. You can be like God. You can make the rules." *(Back to the sidewalk.)*
FAIRNESS WORKER. Well, yeah, as a matter of fact I am gay. *(Door slams.)* We get that a lot. It might be worse today because we're interrupting the Broncos game. Me? I'm a Celtic Wiccan. I grew up in a Christian family, but we never really went to church; the closest I got was Exodus International, which was like living in a church … What? Oh it's like straight camp, it's where you go to recover from being a homosexual. ANYTHING is possible if you believe in Jesus enough. They even showed us straight porn, like to say, this is what you should like, but … yeah but then if you like it too much I'm sure they'd send you off to porn camp.
FAIRNESS LEADER. Oh, I know where you should go! This church here around the corner, Emmanuel Baptist, it's the biggest black church in Colorado Springs. The pastor's name's Ben Reynolds. He said to his congregation, "I want to sign on as a supporter of Referendum I, but I won't do it without you." *(Question.)* No. They're pretty evenly divided. Just go over there: Ben Reynolds, Emmanuel Baptist. It's right there.

Scene 7

Emmanuel Baptist

Near the altar at Emmanuel Baptist. The Emmanuel Choir Member, an older African-American woman.

EMMANUEL CHOIR MEMBER. So. You want to know about Emmanuel? You know I sing in the sanctuary choir. I get up there and I'm directing the choir. And what's hurt this church was that Pastor Reynolds was bringing in a lot of homosexuals and putting 'em up on that pulpit saying "Oh, they anointed by God." And I kept saying, "Lord, something's not right here. Something's not right." And it was eating at my spirit inside. So that's when I really started praying, asking God to reveal it. "God, clean this mess up." Those were my words to the Lord. Everything that is being hid here for a long time, let there be no more suspicions on anything.

So then this one evening, Pastor Reynolds said he wanted the whole choir to come back after the last service, to sing for *another* service to support the AIDS ministry. And I look out in the audience and I say, "Oh, we ain't got a lot a Emmanuel members out there. We got a lot of whites. And they homosexuals." So where the cross is, they had fifty candles on the table, and they said ya'll come up and burn a candle for somebody you know done died a AIDS. So I'm looking at them, "Yup, you gay. Yup, you gay. Yup, you gay." Ain't none of them members from here. *(T-Girl Christian enters and lights a candle.)* But what blew me away was Over-Six-Foot Blondie. I call him Over-Six-Foot Blondie. He was dressed in women clothing. He had on this long blonde wig. This dress. And I looked at his feet. And I looked over where Reynolds was and I looked at the choir and I looked at everyone up there onstage and I said, "Holy Spirit, don't tell me I'm the only one up here that recognize that's a man dressed as a woman." I said, "Holy Spirit, I know I'm not the only one up here that recognize that that's a man dressed as a woman." *(Starts to laugh.)* I guess I'm the only one that sees this.

T-GIRL CHRISTIAN. Oh, we trans girls are in the basement of the basement. And here, most people don't even understand what it is to be transsexual; they just think we're drag queens that won't quit. And the gay community doesn't like us 'cause they think we are sell-outs 'cause we want to be girls. Then on the opposite side, the lesbians *(Blows air through lips.)* because you ain't one of us *(Makes vampire cross with fingers.)* Oh no! Even if I was post-op, and had all the "whoop-de-doo." So it's like living in the middle of nowhere, and you have no people and no country, and that is what it's like.

And well, living in this city … *(Question.)* No, I was not out, when I came to Colorado Springs. I was married, had a wife and two kids and we were very conservative Christians. We joined one of these big churches. We became small group leaders. We did all that. And a lot of those people at Focus on the Family. I was their Sunday school teacher! *(Laughs.)* And yes, I was against the LGBT community. I was like Ted Haggard, more or less. I was saying, "That's sin." Until my mind got expanded, and I faced up to all the bad I was doing to my own community — that's something I'm doing penance for now and will never be able to pay back.

Now, the vast majority of LGBT people have turned away from God. They've been so hurt by their church that they say if that's how their God is, then I don't want no part of him. Some Christians will be nice and say, "Well, God would accept you as you are, but he's too kind to leave you this way." Yes, and that's their nice way of saying that you need to change. And I'm like, "Sorry. Been there, done that. Bought that T-shirt, burnt it and bought a blouse!"

But I almost walked away from God. I was gone for a long time, almost nine months. Because I didn't think God could love someone like me. But then there was a friend of mine, she's a T-girl and her name is Katherine, and it's funny 'cause her last name really is Paradise. Katherine Paradise. And she showed me this website: *(Projection: Grace and Lace Letter International. An Evangelical Christian Newsletter for Crossdressers, Transgendered and Transsexuals.)*

And it brought forth arguments from Scripture — and I said, this is great! I can still be a Christian! And it lit me up! And that ended my nine months away from God. I said, I don't have to run anymore! You know what? Why should I? These conservative people are renegades, and they have hijacked the ship of Christianity and they are heading it towards the rocks!

Scene 8

An Email from Ted

Song: An Email from Ted. The song can be sung by an actor playing Haggard, a character reading the email, a voiceover, etc.

SINGER.
FROM: TED.HAGGARD@NEWLIFECHURCH.ORG
DEAR NEW LIFE CHURCH,
YESTERDAY A SMALL TEAM OF EVANGELICAL LEADERS AND
  MYSELF MET WITH BENJAMIN NETANYAHU
AND IN TWO HOURS WE'LL MEET PRIME MINISTER ARIEL
  SHARON.
THEN WE'RE HEADING BACK TO THE UNITED STATES.
BUT I WANTED YOU TO SEE THIS EMAIL ABOUT SOME
  UPCOMING MEDIA ATTENTION
SO YOU CAN HELP ME.
BARBARA WALTERS IS WORKING ON A STORY ABOUT HEAVEN
AND WILL INTERVIEW ME
AND GET SOME SUPPORTING SHOTS FROM THE CHURCH.
SINCE WE BELIEVE IN HEAVEN, WE ARE, IN FACT, A GOOD
  SOURCE.
OK, TOMORROW WE HAVE A MEETING IN WASHINGTON,
THEN ON FRIDAY WE'LL FLY TO NEW YORK
TO APPEAR ON *THE O'REILLY FACTOR.*
THEN WE'LL ZIP HOME TO BE WITH YOU ON SUNDAY.
SAINTS, I NEED YOUR STRENGTH.
I LOVE YOU!
AND I LOVE BEING YOUR PASTOR,
LOVE, TED

Scene 9

Air Force Academy

TRAILS GUIDE #2. Campfires are an outdoor tradition, but if mishandled, can cause great damage — and sometimes burn down the whole forest. So if you make a fire, make it small. They're easier to put out. *(Three Air Force cadets being interviewed together at the Air Force Academy.)*

CADET C. There's not one group, there's tons of Christian groups that meet here at the Air Force Academy.

CADET A. Yeah, like FCA — Fellowship for Christian Athletes, The Navigators, Campus Crusade for Christ, YWAM — that's Youth With a Mission —

CADET B. And tonight after this, there's God Chasers.

CADET C. And a lot of cadets go to New Life on Friday nights. It's just on the other side of the highway and they send buses.

CADET A. I actually came to Colorado Springs originally to do the missions training program at New Life, and from there it was kind of a natural move for me to come here. I absolutely believe that God needs people in every part of society. Having graduated from the Air Force Academy will give me a huge platform to be able to influence other people's lives through God. *(Question.)*

CADET C. Tonight? Well tonight I think we're talking about the right way to share our faith with others.

CADET B. That means like … well, we call it the good news. I don't know. People do reject Christ on occasion but it doesn't need to be ugly, like, you can still be friends with them. Jesus was friends with sinners. We are called to be their friends and try to make them eternal friends. That's *why* we're friends with them.

CADET C. But here at the Academy it is, uh, a sensitive environment, like a few years ago there was a religious intolerance scandal —

CADET A. But a lot of the stuff that, that they were accusing evangelicals of at the Academy were things that evangelicals had nothing to do with.

CADET B. It wasn't necessarily someone trying to convey the Gospel of Christ —

CADET C. No one here would say "you f-ing Christ killer, you blah blah blah," I mean, no one, we're not gonna do that.

CADET B. We don't even think that.

CADET C. The Romans killed Jesus.

CADET A. But I think there would be a lot less conflict if we were allowed to just openly discuss things. Just talk like we're doing now. But we can't talk about it, because, uh, there are legal issues involved and that has a lot to do with, uh, Mikey Weinstein in particular,

CADET B. Who's the father —

CADET A. Of a cadet here. *(The Military Activist enters. He is in a different location.)*

MIKEY WEINSTEIN. Look, I don't know what you're going for with your show, if you're shooting for G or PG, 'cause with me you're going to get the R version and maybe some X. OK? OK. So, for the record, I was Air Force, one son is still at the Academy in Colorado Springs. All my kids are Air Force. And, you know, I spent fourteen years in, so in my immediate family, we have a hundred and fifteen years' combined active military service. So, um, I think I know a little of what I'm talking about. And let me tell you, the line between the church and the state's armed forces has been completely dissolved. Go back to your hometown paper and read the July 12, 2005 front page of the *New York Times*. General Richardson, the number two ranking chaplain in the Air Force, makes an astonishing fucking statement. Front page *New York Times*. It's the Air Force's official policy to evangelize anyone who comes into the service who is "unchurched." You know, my wife and I have three kids in the U.S. Air Force. And we're Jewish. Now, do our kids fall in this category of being unchurched? And if so, Air Force, are you going to exercise your fucking right to evangelize them?

CADET A. Now, evangelicals messed up their *tactics* tons of times.

CADET C. Yeah, some people have gotten outside the love. Because to evangelize someone shouldn't be just "I'm right and you're wrong and you need to do this." Rather than, "Dude, I love you, and here's the truth, man, and I really love you and I really hope you come to the right decision."

MIKEY WEINSTEIN. And these people would LOVE it. They would just love it if I was some Northern California tree-hugging chardonnay-sipping liberal saying all this but I'm not, I'm a Republican. I was an advisor to Reagan as an attorney, counsel to Ross Perot — am I going too fast? You know that scene in *From Here to Eternity* where Burt Lancaster and Deborah Kerr are rolling in the surf and the water's rushing up over them, that's what I'm doing. I'm just rushing up over you here, I'm just rushing water, you don't have to get every word, OK? Now this evangelical problem, it's not just the Air Force Academy. It's the Marine Corps, Navy, Army. It's our leaders IN THE PENTAGON. So when these guys in the Pentagon talk about Afghanistan, Iraq, they are not talking about it in geopolitical terms, because that is not how they see it. They see it through the book of Revelation, which is a great five-act drama the only problem is my people don't make it past the fourth act. I mean, it's supposed to be the fucking Pentagon, not the Pentecostagon.

CADET A. And really I think now it's almost like you get in trouble for practicing your Christian faith. People just need to calm down and realize, you know, that Christians are gonna be here, and we would never proselytize, but we reserve the right to evangelize to the unchurched. I mean, that's a part of our religion.

MIKEY WEINSTEIN. Look, I have no interest in denying anyone their warm Jesus teddy bear. *Because I do not care what they believe.* Even though these are people that believe that Jack Benny, Dr. Seuss, Gandhi, and Anne Frank are burning in an eternal fiery lake of hell. And hey, if you want to believe that little thirteen-year-old girl who walked into a hermetically sealed gas chamber and whose little pink body was turned into a blue-and-purple polka-dotted corpse, before they shoved it in the crematorium and burned it to cinders, if you want to believe that she's roasting in hell, I'll support, with my last fiber of my being under our social contract of the U.S. Constitution, *your right to believe that.* But if you try to engage in the power of the state, and in the armed forces, and have my government tell me who are the children of the greater god and who are the children of the lesser god, I will fucking kill you or I will go down trying. I am in this battle to the end and I am not finished until I leave a sucking chest wound in each and every one of the Christian Taliban because that is all they understand!!!

Scene 10

End Times

Song: End Times.

WOMAN.
    THE CRAZY WEATHER
    I THINK THIS CRAZY WEATHER IS DEFINITELY A SIGN
    INCREASE IN KNOWLEDGE
    THAT'S TALKED ABOUT IN BOOK OF REVELATION
    AND THE WARS
    THERE'S A WAR IN THE SPIRIT REALM
    I CAN SEE IT

THE CLOCK IS TICKING
THE CLOCK IS TICKING
SOMETHING'S COMING
SOMETHING'S COMING

YOU SEE THESE MOVIES
ALL THESE MOVIES
WHERE NEW YORK IS COVERED IN ICE
OR A TIDAL WAVE
ALL THESE DISASTERS
PEOPLE HAVE SEEN THIS STUFF
SO WHEN THEY LOOK OUT THEIR WINDOW AND SEE
A PLAGUE OF LOCUSTS
A PLAGUE OF FROGS
THE COAST OF CALIFORNIA COVERED IN BLOOD
IT'S NOT GONNA FREAK PEOPLE OUT THAT MUCH

THE CLOCK IS TICKING
THE CLOCK IS TICKING
SOMETHING'S COMING
SOMETHING'S COMING
IT'S SO EXCITING
BECAUSE GOD IS RAISING UP A NEW GENERATION
AND WE FEEL LIKE CHRISTMAS IS COMING
BUT GIVE ME ONE MORE DAY
GIVE ME ONE MORE HOUR
TO SAVE ANOTHER SOUL
'CAUSE THERE'S NOT MUCH TIME
'TIL THE TIME ARRIVES
WHEN THE BATTLE IS WON
WHEN MY FATHER WILL SHOW ME WHAT MY LIFE IS FOR
THAT THERE IS MORE TO COME THAN WE COULD EVER KNOW
YES THERE IS MORE TO COME THAN WE COULD EVER KNOW
GIVE ME ONE MORE DAY
GIVE ME ONE MORE HOUR
END TIMES ARE COMING
END TIMES ARE COMING

Scene 11

Spiritual Warfare

At home with Young Woman, in her kitchen.

YOUNG WOMAN — GOD'S GRACE. We came from a Christian background. My father's father was a minister, so it was really a shock for all of us when my dad came out of the closet. So after my parents divorced, I moved out here to live with my dad, actually. I was just a kid and I wanted my dad, you know? I wanted him to keep loving me. But then my dad's boyfriend moved in. And I was put on the back burner; he didn't need me. So I just went wild and did whatever I wanted to. I actually met my husband when I'd just turned sixteen and within a few months I was living with him. My dad was like, whatever! A week after I turned seventeen, my dad signed for us to get married, and then left for California. Yeah, my dad left right after. Really fast right after. *(Kids in the distant background.)* Guys. Keep it down, please. Anyhow, my husband and I lived over in Manitou Springs then. *(A little quieter.)* There was constant drug use, for lack of a better way to put it. I can probably count the days of sobriety on two hands. My husband and I had a really short bout with crystal meth. And it must have been the grace of God, 'cause I've heard that it's really hard to get off of. And the day before, a Saturday night, my husband and I were actually at a strip club, and we were doing coke with a bunch of strippers — I dunno, it was a party night. We had a babysitter. And I guess I had just been very gently hearing God calling to me, because the next morning I got up, and I got the kids dressed, and I walked them to this church down the road, Revolution Church. Just like that, and it was funny. I mean, look where I'd been just a few hours before. And Revolution was unlike anything I had ever been to. They had like strobe lights and a smoke machine and a disco ball! And the people there were my age and they had tattoos! And I was sitting there with my boys, and I felt that I just didn't realize that I had missed God! And I said, "God, who am I to you?" And he just revealed to me, "You are my daughter. You are the one who pleases me." And in a way it made me ashamed. But at the same time he just lifted that burden off of me. He freed me, and just revealed to me that it was OK. And it made his heart ache every time I made a poor choice, but he loved me nonetheless, and he wasn't willing to let me

32

go. *(Wipes away tears.)* To think of where I was four years ago. Now I can see how selfish that life was, and today I'm just so thankful. But at the same time, there is this sadness that washes over me because, the clock is ticking and we need more time. Like, I used to work as a senior companion, and I worked for this gentleman for a few years. And I got the call one day that he had died, and it just, really to this day, I regret that I never … that I was too afraid to say anything about his salvation. I have a really vivid imagination. And to think of him in terror, and in hell for the rest of all eternity … He was such a beautiful man. *(Wipes away tears.)* I'm sorry, when God is consuming me I just start to leak.

You know it's funny, that day if I had just walked into some boring church, I would still be sitting on the couch smoking pot. We really liked Revolution and are still really good friends with the leaders, but it went from being a church to being a twenty-four-hour house of prayer. Just prayer. All the time. By the time we left it had gone from like a hundred and fifty members to twelve or something. Yeah, Revolution House of Prayer. RHOP, right. Oh, you've been there? What did you think? *(We go to RHOP, a house of prayer headquartered in a small office building. We meet an RHOP member, a woman with a dramatic blonde hairstyle and striking eye makeup, and the RHOP leader, a man in his late thirties.)*

RHOP MEMBER. Oh gosh *(Laughs.)* I'm not good at interviews. What am I doing here? *(Laughs.)*

RHOP LEADER. So of all the churches you've been to is this one by far the most bizarre?

RHOP MEMBER. You don't think we're weird? We're more down-to-earth than you probably think. I don't think of myself as a religious freak, I just never have. But if I see a woman in your play with a big bee hairdo and Tammy Faye make-up, I'm going to know it's me.

RHOP LEADER. Now we're … well obviously we're not a church like New Life. We're more like Special Forces. See, here at RHOP, we're all about revival. Hey, if you guys can come back next week, we're going to do a revival night. We're going to do some worship here and then we're headed for an intensive session in the cave. We take everyone into this cave for about four hours, it's pitch black, you can totally come if you like. *(Interviewer declines.)* OK. You can decide later.

RHOP MEMBER. But you can just come around for the first part here, you can observe and see what we do. *(Interviewer responds.)* Oh … you know if you're going to be talking to Christians, you really shouldn't say you want to be a fly on the wall. That's Beelzebub. *(Laughs.)* Yeah, Lord of the Flies. He sneaks in as a fly on the wall. So you don't want to say that.

RHOP LEADER. So what Ted Haggard did in Colorado Springs in the nineties — city transformation, do you know what that means? OK — well, that's what we're trying to do here. And what I see here for Manitou Springs is the entire city as a church. I know it sounds impossible, but God's given us a vision of a church that encompasses the whole city. *(Question.)* You mean are there people who wouldn't like that to happen? That's why the warfare is necessary. *(Question.)* Huh? Well, bombs and missiles. *(Big laugh.)* No, just kidding. It's not like that at all. It's spiritual warfare.

RHOP MEMBER. Yeah, people misunderstand our rhetoric. What we MEAN is that we're praying and the violence is in the spiritual realm.

RHOP LEADER. Right, the idea is that, if we could see with spiritual eyes, we would see demons, you know, wherever, at Starbucks.

RHOP MEMBER. And see, the spiritual realm is so much more intense than the physical realm. I've been to meetings where this one lady started levitating, she's like this high up off the floor and we're trying to do a service. See that's a fear spirit at work. It's using her to distract us from the service. Well, I got angry. So I walked over and picked her up and threw her in a chair. She's like "What happened!" and I go, "You were levitating!" *(Laughs.)* And not everyone can see into the spirit realm, but I see things — they're real, they're just invisible to most people. The other day, I saw this huge, it looked like a black bull, and it had like a greasy body. And this thing, I don't know how it got on him, had its claws in this little boy's head. So I had to pull the thing off of him and set the boy free.

RHOP LEADER. And these demons influence mankind. They influence the way a city is run. Most churches here fail in their first two years. Because the spiritual resistance is incredible. And I believe it will probably intensify when — talking kingdom of God stuff, when the kingdom of God is established, there will be people, more than likely, unless everyone gets saved, which I would love that, that really just won't like it. And that's a tough thing. But I know this, I know God owns this city, and he's not able to dwell here. *(Emmanuel Choir Member back at her interview at Emmanuel.)*

EMMANUEL CHOIR MEMBER. You got Satan in the pulpit. Well you let Satan up there 'cause he entertaining you. Well, I had already started. Way over a year ago. Paying attention, always paid attention to what's going on in the pulpit. And then — Pastor Reynolds, he gets up there and he make his announcement and he tells us that he's homosexual, and he's coming up with all kinda justification for people to accept his lifestyle. Well, I'm sick of your lifestyle. When you wanna take your lifestyle and goin' throw it on somebody, and gonna make demand somebody accept you — and tell us that we should be supporting this, this, this, Referendum. Demand somebody give you a health right — give you a — you ain't entitled to nothing! Because I'll tell you exactly wh-what I know and what I been taught is the word of God. It is one man, one woman. And you will never change that. So we put Reynolds out. But you put 'em out as Christian who has strayed. And he belongs to Satan. And while he's at Satan, the Lord is hoping he will change himself before the time end and he will come back. When that person repent. We are to restore them back. But after I read it in the paper. With his picture on the front page. Front page! I WILL NOT REPENT. OK. See ya. Hello, Satan. 'Cause if you do not repent, oh, you goin' to hell, homeboy. *(Song: Demons.)*

    THERE ARE DEMONS ALL AROUND
    AND THEY'RE WALKING NEXT TO YOU
    SO MANY DEMONS ALL AROUND
    AND THEY KNOW YOUR WEAKNESS
    THEY KNOW YOUR WEAKNESS
    MY SON IS SCREAMING IN THE MIDDLE OF THE NIGHT
    MAMA MAMA IT'S RIGHT THERE!
    RIGHT THERE! RIGHT THERE!
    HE SEES A DEMON IN THE MIDDLE OF THE NIGHT
    IT WAS TRYING TO KILL HIM, IT WANTS TO TAKE HIM

GROUP A.
    OH, WHAT CAN WE DO
    WHAT CAN WE DO
    TO CAST THE DEVIL OUT
    CONTINUE TO PRAY IN JESUS' NAME
    WE SAY TO YOU BE GONE NOW

GROUP B.
    SPIRITS OF WILL
    SPIRITS OF PRESENCE,
    SPIRITS OF SPEECH,
    SPIRITS OF KNOWLEDGE,
    SPIRITS OF STEALTH
    SPIRITS OF ANGER
    SPIRITS OF LUST
    SPIRITS PERVERTED.
    SPIRITS OF LOVE.
    SPIRITS OF DEATH

    THERE WAS A GIRL ON A PRAYER RETREAT
    INTO WITCHCRAFT AND THE DARK
    WE WERE PRAYING FOR DELIVERANCE
    FROM THE DEMON IN THIS GIRL

THE HOLY SPIRIT OF THE LORD IT HIT SO HARD
THAT THE GIRL FELL ON THE GROUND
I HEARD THE SPIRIT OF THE DEMON CRYING OUT
"YOU'VE INVITED ME, THIS IS MY HOME, MY HOME, MY HOME"
GROUP B. *(Under the following texts.)*
SPIRITS OF WILL
SPIRITS OF PRESENCE,
SPIRITS OF SPEECH,
SPIRITS OF KNOWLEDGE,
SPIRITS OF STEALTH
SPIRITS OF ANGER
SPIRITS OF LUST
SPIRITS PERVERTED.
SPIRITS OF LOVE.
SPIRITS OF DEATH.
RHOP LEADER. A lot of people just think spiritual warfare as, "Oh, I pray and the Devil goes away." But it is a very real battle. And in battles there are casualties. So, it's a war. It's God versus the Devil and that's the way it's been since the foundation of the earth.

NEW LIFE ASSOCIATE PASTOR. OK, New Life, as a kingdom-minded people we don't have the luxury to not care about politics. God needs you to walk the walk because this mid-term election is an opportunity to defend God's plan for marriage. And God has given us the tools to win this battle. It's simple. Register and vote. People, God asks missionaries to go work for him in the darkest corners of the earth. He asks the young men and women of this country to serve him in Iraq and Afghanistan. And right now all he's asking you to do is vote. Are you going to tell him no?

EMMANUEL CHOIR MEMBER. My prayers had been that anything evil that stands in the pulpit, I don't care where they at. Lord, let them be exposed. And then the next week. The next week! I hear the gay guy on the radio. Coming outta Denver. And he's saying he had a, a three-year relationship with some pastor "right down there at Colorado Springs!" He wouldn't call his name. And I'm thinking, you ain't exposing Reynolds. He was already in the paper. So you must be talking about another new one. And then he says "He's big. Like president of something." So I knew it. He was talking about someone at New Life.

End of Act One

ACT TWO

Scene 1

TRAILS GUIDE #3. With the proper precautions, and a solid plan, the hiker who reaches the top of Pike's Peak is well-rewarded for the effort. But in the euphoria of having reached the summit, with its panoramic vistas of Colorado Springs and the plains stretched out eight thousand feet below, don't forget you are only at the half-way point of your journey. You still have to get back down.

Revelations

RHOP revival. A male member of RHOP by himself. Song: Doubting Thomas.

MALE RHOP MEMBER.
    THE DEVIL HAS A MAP
    AND THERE IS NOTHING THAT CAN HIDE YOU
    AND YOUR SCARS WILL REVEAL ALL THE SECRETS YOU TRY TO
        KEEP HIDDEN

    YOUR BODY IS A TRAP
    THERE IS A TICKING BOMB INSIDE YOU
    CAN YOU FREE YOURSELF FROM THE THINGS YOU KNOW ARE
        FORBIDDEN

    WHEN THE DEVIL SEES YOUR WOUNDS
    AND HE TEMPTS YOU IN THE DARK
    IF YOU FOLLOW HIM HE SAYS
    HE'LL NEVER EXPOSE YOU
    'CAUSE HE KNOWS YOU

SO ARE YOU READY
ARE YOU READY TO SAY

LET THERE BE NOTHING HIDDEN IN MY LIFE
I DON'T WANT ANY SECRETS IN MY LIFE
LET THERE BE NO DARKNESS IN MY LIFE

RHOP LEADER. *(Speaking at a microphone.)* OK, first off I want to welcome those of you who are coming to RHOP for your first revival. We're gonna worship here for a bit and then we'll be ready to go to the cave. OK, second thing is we've got some visitors here from New York City. They've come back just to see what we do, so welcome them. OK. Let's get started. We say to any demonic stronghold in anyone's life right now you must break … you must break … in Jesus' name you cannot remain you cannot control in Jesus' name we declare freedom. OK. *(Gesturing to the mic.)* OK, come up, anyone come up. Holy holy holy.

RHOP MEMBER. Lord God we ask that you bring light to this city. Lord God, we welcome your revelations. We are listening, Lord God, we are waiting for your direction. We praise you, Lord God. *(Speaking in tongues/prayer language.)* *Avvon d- Nih- Oo' mal-choota-oo khai-tush-al-mein!* Amen, Lord God.

RHOP LEADER. *(To everyone.)* I'm feeling God urging us to a place of understanding that in order to light this city He's giving me a picture ooh-aah He's giving me a picture of a city and it's night and all of a sudden you can just see just quadrants of the city, and lights are coming on in the homes, and the streetlights are coming on, there had been a blackout and it's just all of a sudden the lights are coming on. *(Online sound. Projection: HAGGARD ACCUSED and a chat icon indicating that we've jumped outside the revival into the Haggard story unfolding online.)*

ONLINE CHATTER. Oh my God! One week before the election, and this is delivered in a nicely ribboned holiday gift box. Looks like Ted Haggard is a closet case and a meth queen to boot! Apparently he's been getting it on with this Denver hooker named Mike Jones and scoring speed. In the words of Whitney Houston: Merry Crystal-meth-mas! Check this out: *(Actors switch out of their RHOP characters and play Haggard and a reporter interviewing him in the driveway outside of his home.)*

REPORTER. Pastor Haggard, have you had a relationship with —

TED HAGGARD. I have not.

REPORTER. Any kind of gay relationship —

TED HAGGARD. I, I've never had a gay relationship with anybody and, uh, I, I'm steady with my wife. I'm faithful to my wife.

REPORTER. What about the accusations you tried to buy meth?

TED HAGGARD. I have never done drugs, ever. Not even in high school.
REPORTER. Uh. So you don't know Mike Jones?
TED HAGGARD. No, I do not know Mike Jones. *(Back at the revival.)*
RHOP MEMBER. *(Praying with someone at the revival.)* Lord God, don't hold back, this man is strong, give him all you got. Give it to him, he can take it.
RHOP LEADER. I have a picture for you. When the flesh dies there's this amazing release and that's what God wants for you now. He wants you to die in the flesh so you can feel that freedom. He wants that for you right now. So just let go and fall back fall back fall back into his arms. *(Back to the news. This time a reporter is interviewing Ted, who has stopped his car. Gayle Haggard sits in the passenger seat.)*
HAGGARD. So, I've put myself on an extended … What do we call it — suspension of my senior pastor's role. I resigned as president from the National Association of Evangelicals because both of those roles are based on trust. And right now my trust is questionable. And so …
REPORTER. The voice expert that is in Denver that was hired by KUSA has …
HAGGARD. Yes.
REPORTER. … matched now eighteen of the words left on the voicemail message.
HAGGARD. Yes. I did call him. I did call him.
REPORTER. And what did you call him about?
HAGGARD. I called him to buy some meth, but I threw it away.
REPORTER. So you now admit you know Mike Jones?
HAGGARD. Uh — I went to him for — I went there for a massage. So — OK, we're late for our appointment. So — but thank you for your work. *(Back at the revival.)*
RHOP LEADER. OK, OK, OK, stay with me here. Now in the cave it's gonna be totally dark, totally silent. We'll be there for about four hours but before we go I want to tell you some of the amazing things that can happen in the cave. This one time — now first you gotta imagine, it's a cave. And you can't see anybody. So there I was, and all of a sudden I saw a demon. And all it was was two red eyes. And and I said "All right guys, I need you to renounce this spirit! Are you ready to break through this thing?" And they were:
ALL. Yes, yes, yes.
RHOP LEADER. I said, "This is what you need to do, everyone of you has to cry out to God." And man … talk about a *change* 'cause it was: *(The revival has morphed into a recreation of the RHOP Leader's story.)*
ALL. "DEVIL YOU GET OUTTA MY LIFE!" "GET OUT OF MY LIFE! GET OUT GET OUT GET OUT GET OUT GET OUT! GOD I NEED

YOU! COME GOD COME! COME! COME!" *(Projection: TED HAGGARD FIRED. Emmanuel Choir Member reappears.)*
EMMANUEL CHOIR MEMBER. I said "Thank ya, Holy Spirit." 'Cause that was my prayer. Expose them! Cause I'm sick of them hiding behind your cloth. No. I ain't jumping for joy for none of 'em to fall, I'm jumping for joy that God restored my faith. Seeing his miracles work today! Dang all these miracles are happening and stuff. Every day!

Scene 2

New Life Church

At New Life worship service. This is the day after Ted Haggard's removal from the church, and only a few days after the scandal broke. The New Life band plays music.

TAG PASTOR. We've had a wonderful twenty-one years here at New Life Church. Pastor Ted said many times that we've been living a little slice of Heaven. For the last couple days we've been living a little slice of Hell, but Heaven! Is! Our! Home! And if we all stay together, praise the Holy Spirit, and continue our work in this city, then we have another twenty years and more, I believe with all of my heart that New Life Church's best days are ahead of us!

In the words of Pastor Ted: What is the purpose of New Life Church? To make it hard to go to Hell in Colorado Springs. So let's turn this room into a house of prayer tonight. Cry out for this church, cry out on behalf of the believers all over the nation who are wrestling with the same demons. Oh God, we bow our hearts to you! Lord Jesus we ask you to purge our hearts, to take all judgmental thoughts away. All bitterness! All anger! All fear! God, we are so desperate for you, would you come, would you come and save us? Rescue us LORD JESUS! GOD!!! *(Song: Take Me There.)*
> THE EYES OF A NATION,
> THE ENTIRE WORLD IS WATCHING
> THE REVELATION OF A
> NEW AGE THAT IS DAWNING
> A NEW AGE THAT IS DAWNING.

WHAT IS THE PLAN FOR
THIS PLACE, THIS TOWN, THIS CITY?
WHO IS THE MAN FOR THE
NEW AGE THAT IS DAWNING,
THE NEW AGE THAT IS DAWNING?

WHERE YOU WILL GO TAKE ME ALONG,
TELL ME SHOW ME WHAT I'VE DONE WRONG
TO YOU I DEDICATE THIS SONG.

TO SOMEONE UP ABOVE
WE LIFT OUR VOICE IN PRAYER
PLEASE FILL US WITH YOUR LOVE AND TAKE US THERE,
I KNOW YOU'LL TAKE ME THERE!

ASSOCIATE PASTOR. God is not intimidated by sin. He has an incredible plan. And you're seeing it, you're watching it unfold, you're watching the Gospel at work, it is his plan and he will not let us go. Today salvation is working!

WE HAVE A VISION
WE SEE THE PASSAGE IN THE NIGHT
WE HAVE A MISSION
TO BRING THE CITY INTO LIGHT
BRING THE CITY INTO LIGHT.

I KNEW A STORY
I THOUGHT THAT I HAD HEARD THE PLAN
TO SHOW YOUR GLORY
BUT DID WE REALLY UNDERSTAND?
DID WE REALLY UNDERSTAND?

WHERE YOU WILL GO TAKE ME ALONG,
TELL ME SHOW ME WHAT I'VE DONE WRONG
TO YOU I DEDICATE THIS SONG.

TO SOMEONE UP ABOVE
WE LIFT OUR VOICE IN PRAYER
PLEASE FILL US WITH YOUR LOVE AND TAKE US THERE,
I KNOW YOU'LL TAKE ME THERE!

(The following speech is a voiceover or somehow outside of the scene. Haggard is not

present.)

TED HAGGARD. *(A letter.)* My Dear New Life Church Family, I am sorry for the betrayal, and the hurt. The fact is there is a part of my life that is so repulsive and dark that I have been warring against it all of my adult life. For periods of time, I would rejoice in freedom. Then the dirt would resurface, and I would experience desires that were contrary to everything I believe. But I am responsible; I alone need to be disciplined. I know this situation will put you to the test. I'm sorry I've created the test, but please rise to this challenge and demonstrate the incredible grace that is available to all of us.

I KNOW YOU'LL TAKE ME THERE.
I KNOW YOU'LL TAKE ME THERE.
I KNOW YOU'LL TAKE ME,
YOU'LL TAKE ME,
YOU'LL TAKE ME THERE.
I KNOW YOU'LL TAKE ME THERE.
I KNOW YOU'LL TAKE ME THERE.
I KNOW YOU'LL TAKE ME,
YOU'LL TAKE ME,
YOU'LL TAKE ME.

TO SOMEONE UP ABOVE
WE LIFT OUR VOICE IN PRAYER
PLEASE FILL US WITH YOUR LOVE AND TAKE US THERE.

Scene 3

Reverberations

The Alt Writer has entered at the end of "Take Me There." He opens a copy of his newspaper and reads from his own editorial.

ALT WRITER. "Don't get me wrong: I was as surprised as anyone that Haggard actually got caught. Just because everyone knows you're a repressed hypocritical piece of shit doesn't necessarily mean you're stupid enough to get caught. But those of us who live in Colorado Springs knew something was up. And we knew

because the church itself told us everything Haggard was hiding. If you've been to New Life and have even trace amounts of gaydar, then it doesn't come as any surprise that Ted Haggard turned out to be a meth-fueled queerbag. When my big gay stepdad saw him on the news for the first time three years ago, his first comment was: 'Well he's as gay as a box of birds.'" *(He closes the newspaper.)* A lot of people criticized my paper for gloating about his fall. I mean, of course, the guy's obviously tortured. I feel for his kids certainly, having grown up with the shame that I grew up with having two queer parents, you know, *until I got over it.* But they're the ones who made this political and you know, when they slip, you wanna slide a little bed of nails underneath as they're going down. *(Online.)*
VOICEOVER. You must be logged in to leave a comment. Would you like to sign in now? *(Bloggers and online comments.)*
BROOKE. I don't know about the rest of you, but this was one of the best weekends ever. I could watch Ted's confession on YouTube for the rest of my life and never stop smiling. I heard just now that Dobson is going to counsel him to stop his gay tendencies. OK, dude, go ahead, make someone NOT gay. — Posted by Brooke, Boulder.
DERRICK. I just went to the New Life website, checked out the all-male staff and all these guys look like Liberace with a buzz cut. Anyone know if Mike Jones outing Ted is affecting the gay marriage vote in Colorado? — Derrick, Cleveland.
BOBBY. I hear the vote in Colorado is pretty close. But what I think will be truly fascinating to observe is how the right-wingers react to this news about Ted. Will there be a call for unity or will they throw him to the wolves? — Bobby, Pittsburgh.
BROOKE. Bobby, click here:
CNN.COM. White House spokesperson Tony Fratto downplayed the pastor's connections to the Bush administration.
FRATTO. He had been on a couple of conference calls but was not a weekly participant in those calls.
CNN.COM. Fratto admitted that Haggard had been to the White House.
FRATTO. One or two times. But there have been a lot of people who come to the White House.
BROOKE. Does that answer your question, Bobby? *(They exit.)*
YOUNG WOMAN — GOD'S GRACE. When I first found out about Pastor Ted, I was shopping in town and my husband sent me a text message and I just stopped right in the middle of the aisle, and I felt cold rush over me from head to toe, and I texted my husband, saying, it can't be true, can it? But when I got home and went online and listened to the tapes of his phone calls, it was him — it was the message about how he wanted to go up to Denver and pick up some

more "stuff." He was using total drug lingo and I know! You know? I used to make those calls! He wanted two hundred dollars' worth, and I remember thinking, "Whoa, that's a lot of meth! It's a cheap drug! That's a lot lot lot!"

But through all of this not once have I felt like New Life was falling apart. The other day, my neighbor called me flipping out, "I've got to get my children re-baptized, I've got to get them re-baptized" and I was like, "Why?" And she said "Because Pastor Ted baptized them!" And I'm like, what does that have to do with anything?

Maybe it was more for other people to deal with than it was for me. Because I've been dealing with this all my life. 'Cause I remember the nights that my mom would keep me up crying about my dad. So my concern was more for Pastor Ted and his family. When you've done nothing but run a church for twenty-plus years … what do you do? Do you get a job at Pizza Hut? *(In Denver.)*

BEN REYNOLDS. You want to know what happened to me at Emmanuel Baptist? Well after I made my announcement, they basically fired me. It was just that cut. Boom. Get outta here. *(Laughs.)* Well, and I'm laughing now, but this thing with Ted Haggard, it's a very sad thing. I just wish that he could have told his own story. Because that's what I did. I am the author. I mean, of course it is still at a price, 'cause here I am a vagabond on the streets of Denver.

But I knew it was coming, ever since I started preaching, I think the crowning jewel that forced my decision was Referendum I. The lack of understanding around it. So I was like, you know what, the next time this congregation thinks of a same-gender-loving African-American male and benefits and rights, maybe I will come to their minds.

But when I made the announcement, one of the leading deacons said to me "I knew it all the time." And that's a very arrogant thing to say when someone tells such a dynamic truth as to expose their sexuality. Because you really don't know anything until a person tells the truth to you. So when I analyzed it, he was saying, "We all knew. But the nerve of you to speak that truth in here. We're angry because you spoke the truth." Because if you knew and I just told you, then really, this ought to be a party. Like, whew, glad that's over with. Now can we move on to something else?

YOUNG WOMAN — GOD'S GRACE. Forgiving my father for what he did to my family is a daily thing. And really, the forgiveness is for me. I need to let go of that anger. But my dad … well he's been so hurt by a lot of quote unquote religious people — like he's had bricks thrown through his window and death threats, because he's a big supporter of gay marriage — that all he can see is "those right-wing freaks." And he's including me in that.

BEN REYNOLDS. So after they kicked me out, I knew I had to leave some dis-

tance between Colorado Springs and me. And here in Denver it's still too close. I mean, I can be walking down the street and like, people have stopped me and they want to talk. And most think, "Oh my God, he's fallen from grace." *(Giggles.)* They don't know how happy I am. They just don't know. I'm like brand new. On a Saturday night, back then, as a pastor, three o'clock I was at home. Shut up with the windows drawn, hahaha, you know, praying honestly for the Word. But now, while I continue to pray, I might be out on a Saturday night with a glass of wine. And I like my life that way. Free. I feel free. And I am gay everywhere. *(Song: Freedom.)*
YOUNG WOMAN — GOD'S GRACE.

YOU WANT YOUR FREEDOM
YOU WANT YOUR CHOICES
YOU WANT THE ABILITY TO LIVE AS YOU CHOOSE

BUT THE ONLY FREEDOM
IS WITH YOUR FAMILY
IN THE SAFETY THAT GOD WILL NEVER REFUSE

I KNOW YOU'RE ANGRY
ABOUT MY CHOICES
I KNOW YOU THINK THAT I MIGHT JUDGE YOU
YOU WALK AWAY FROM GOD
YOU CALL THAT FREEDOM
AND THAT'S THE TEST WE HAVE TO FACE
SO WATCH ME WATCH ME

AND I WILL PRAY
AND I WILL FOLLOW
AND I WILL OBEY
AND I WILL SHOW
THAT I WILL LOVE YOU
AND THAT IS MY CALLING
THAT IS THE FREEDOM THAT I KNOW

ASSOCIATE PASTOR. I don't know anybody who wasn't shocked. When I saw the headline on the computer, early, early, Thursday morning when everything happened, I thought, *"Holy crap."* But now what's most interesting is watching God work through this crisis. I talked to Pastor Ted and Gayle on Monday? Is that right? Monday night? They were very adamant that God is involved in their marriage, very aggressively saying to me, "We are going to do this right." Which doesn't in any way, this doesn't make OK the things that were wrong — but even

in repentance, Ted is modeling how to do it right. How to be authentically sub-
missive to the authority of God.
WITHOUT SUBMISSION
WHAT WILL SUSTAIN YOU
AS YOU LIE THERE AT NIGHT

ARE YOU HAPPY
ARE YOU FREE NOW
DO YOU THINK THINGS ARE ALL RIGHT?

YOU REJECT ME
YOU DON'T NEED ME
THAT'S YOUR FREEDOM

BUT I WILL PRAY
AND I WILL FOLLOW
AND I WILL OBEY
AND I WILL SHOW
THAT I STILL LOVE YOU
AND THAT IS MY CALLING
THAT IS THE FREEDOM THAT I KNOW

Scene 4

Election

Cheering, celebration sounds. Red, white, and blue balloons drop.

A BUCKIN BRONCO FOR RUDY G. The results are in! Apparently Mike
Jones' ploy didn't work, Colorado still voted down the gay rights measure and
God's plan for marriage is now affirmed in the Colorado state constitution. If the
lifestyles of other countries are what some people want, then the true beauty of
our country is that they are free to leave.
HELEN WHEELS. Why the fuck should I care if two gay people want to get
married? But hey, you won on your little wedge issue. Good for you. I am sooo

46

sorry that your party just got hammered across the country. — Posted by Helen Wheels. Get it? Helen-Wheels.

POSTING. The simple lesson is this: The right kind of Democrat can do very well in the Mountain West, and take the electoral votes here to the White House —

A BUCKIN' BRONCO FOR RUDY G. You might have won a few seats in Congress, but look at America. Look at Colorado. You really believe a liberal can win the bigtime? Me, I'm looking forward to an elephant-riding president in '08. — Posted by A Buckin' Bronco for Rudy G!

MR. TOODLES. I'll just contentedly sit here with my majority in both houses. Enjoy the next two years. I know I will. — Posted by Mr. Toodles.

TOODLE-OO. Every great country has its cancer. Our cancer is Democrats, gays, and other spineless liberals. Posted by Toodle-OO.

MR. TOODLES. Oh, put down your Bible and pull your head out of your ass. — Mr. Toodles.

TOODLE-OO. At least gays lost and didn't ruin the fiber of our nation. — Toodle-OO.

MR. TOODLES. The last fiber ruined in this nation *(Start "Roundarado.")* was on Monica's dress. — Mr. Toodles.

ROUNDARADO. It's also because, that we have, and the fact that as Colorado, we're a rectangle. Maybe a square. We should be round. We should be more well-rounded. We should be Roundarado. Do you know what I mean? Roundarado.

MR. TOODLES.
TOODLE-OO
MR. TOODLES
TOODLE-OO
TOODLE-OO
TOODLE-OO
TOODLE-OO

YOU GUYS ARE ALL HATEFUL. I can't believe how hateful you guys are! — Posted by You Guys are All Hateful.

Scene 5

Coffee Shop

FAIRNESS LEADER. Well we lost Referendum I. And they passed the marriage amendment. Yeah. But I — and maybe this is just to save my psyche — but we lost by a narrow margin. Does that satisfy me? Absolutely not. Am I pissed? Absolutely. But I have to find some kernel of solace, some kernel of some kind of germination of social change. I have to see that.

ASSOCIATE PASTOR. This experience … I think I'd compare it to a parent who died early. Somebody who wasn't supposed to have died. So it's been a real test. In twenty years we've been very lucky. And what you learn is that it's a lot easier to have your faith when you haven't been tested. But at a time like this it's different, you really have to remember what you believe because ultimately our faith isn't in a man. It's in God.

MARCUS HAGGARD. New Life has always been home to me. I was one and a half when my dad started New Life in 1985, so I grew up a part of this church. Yeah, I remember when the services were in our basement and my mom would take care of the little kids upstairs.

ASSOCIATE PASTOR. But now … There are days when I feel like "I never want to forgive this guy." No doubt. And other times when I feel like "I want to see my friend." Yeah. *(Question.)* No, I don't think he can be part of this church. Even though we love him. I think the interaction would just be too awkward.

MARCUS HAGGARD. No. I don't think my dad was thinking about politics so much when he started New Life. The people in it just felt, you know, this is who we are — we're political, involved people. *(Question.)* At the height of it all, let's see … I met the president of Israel. He's not that powerful, but … yeah I was in Israel. I was meeting all kinds of crazy people. Billionaires in Indonesia who built churches, but the world my Dad operated in wasn't so interesting to me. It was kind of the world of game-players and pundits.

FAIRNESS LEADER. You know what, we never pay any attention to the evangelicals until it's election time. Then it's suddenly, "Whoa! Who are these people?" And you know what? That's our fault. But honestly, I don't think the Ted thing affected the election one way or the other. Really, it's the other way around. The election brought about Ted's downfall. 'Cause Mike Jones said it was Ted's campaigning for the marriage amendment that made him come forward, so … Yeah, that's getting hoisted by your own petard. *(Laughs.)* Oh, that sounds dirty. I mean, it isn't. *(Laughing.)*

MARCUS HAGGARD. When I first heard the news about my dad, no, didn't see it coming. But at the same time going, "Huh. There could be some truth there." Which was a surprising initial reaction in the face of the accusations. I think it's knowing … there's a lot of interesting stuff in the Haggard family. So there's some of that, "Oh, yeah. That sounds Haggardesque." I haven't fleshed out, like, the homosexual nature of it all, I guess I fall into the traditional camp that it's wrong. I don't think homosexuality is God's perfect intention for his creation, but we don't live in his perfect creation, you know? *(Question.)* The drug thing? I don't know about that. I haven't had that sit down with him yet.

"OK, Dad, what's true and what's not?" But look, I have no problem with him doing what he did. I lost any idea that humans are perfect and don't do these things. I'm sad it went down the way it did. That he got caught and he didn't confess. It's like when a criminal gets caught, and all of a sudden they're like, "Oh, I'm sorry." No you're not! If you hadn't gotten caught you'd still be doing it. But he wasn't ready to confess. For so many years he had this kind of performance going on, this trying to make it all look OK, trying to be like, "I've got it all together," when he didn't. He didn't have it together. It was an act. And the act made him distant. I don't think he realized how distant he had become even from his own kids.

FAIRNESS LEADER. With Ben Reynolds at Emmanuel Baptist at least that church had to deal with him saying, "I'm a gay man." You know? They had to at least see him for who he is. But with Ted, all New Life got was "I'm sick and I need to be cured," and get this: his severance deal with New Life requires one: a gag order, and two: that he move out of Colorado. Forever. Yeah. So to me, the most terrifying thing about all this is how quickly the evangelicals can just make Ted disappear in order to keep the system going.

MARCUS HAGGARD. So, yeah, with my dad it's a fall in one sense in that we view glory as being the top and leading a big church and all those things. *Sure,* tragedy happened there. Flipside is, in my view, my dad's understanding God for the first time. Because, you know, we believe God is unconditional love. He is the *only* one who can love us completely for who we are, no matter what we've done, and heal us. So I think my dad's being healed. I think he's closer to being human now than ever before.

T-GIRL CHRISTIAN. Me, in a way, I was like Haggard more or less. I went through every ex-gay, ex-trans program out there. I went to aversion therapy. They used to make me eat hot sauce if I thought about wearing a dress. But I've known since I was three that I was supposed to be a girl, but something was wrong with the outer package. Before I transitioned to full-time T-girl, I was working at a company here as a civil designer. And I was good at my job. But, oh, I was pushing the limits, going more androgynous, wearing earrings but not like these. *(Shows earrings.)* And finally I was, "Enough is enough! I got to be me." But I was not going to just do shock and awe and show up in my Easter dress. So I called a business meeting, the principals at the company, every significant person. I had handouts. I explained what it is to be transgendered, you know, my life is an open book. My supervisor said you are really brave, I never would have been able to do that. And I said what I need to know from you all is this OK for me to go full-time — it's required for my surgery. They said they needed some time to think, and a week went by and they handed me my pink slip. They couldn't come out and say it per se. I called the labor commission and they said they had no protections for transgendered people. I lost my job, my church, my family, my fortune. I lost everything.

For six months I was getting unemployment, but that's all they ever give you in Colorado, six months. Now only by the grace of the friends of mine, they're propping me up. Otherwise I'd be a bag lady by now. No shit. I'd be out in the street. My vision's horrible. I can't work at McDonalds, because I can hardly read the itty-bitty buttons on the cash register. But when I was at my job, if I had trouble seeing on the computer, I can zoom it up. Plus, designing things, it was just like playing Sim City. Designing parks. Designing roads. I design a neighborhood and then a year later, there it is. They don't know I did it, but there's a warm place in my heart because I helped the city. *(Another actress performs the song. Song: Urban Planning.)*
SINGER.
    YOU DESIGN A NEIGHBORHOOD.
    ONE YEAR LATER THERE IT IS.
    OR A PLACE THAT WAS EMPTY
    NOW A BRIDGE HERE
    A ROAD THERE
    SO YOU MAKE A CITY
    SO YOU BUILD IT GENTLY
    AND YOU SEE THAT WHEN IT GETS DONE
    THERE'S A SIGN HERE
    A PARK THERE
    IT'S PARADISE.
    YES IT'S PARADISE.
    IT'S A PARADISE THAT YOU'VE MADE.
    SO MY DOCTOR SAYS DRAW SOMETHING.
    SO I DRAW A CITY.
    'CAUSE I'VE ALWAYS LIKED CITIES.
    I HAVE SINCE I WAS A KID.
    SO HE TELLS ME IT'S BEAUTIFUL.
    BUT WHERE ARE THE PEOPLE?
    I HAD NEVER THOUGHT OF THE PEOPLE
    THEY MOVE.
    THEY GET IN THE WAY.
    THEY GET IN THE WAY.
    I'M LOOKING AT BUILDINGS.
    HE SAYS THAT'S KIND OF AN ISSUE.
    HAVE PEOPLE HURT YOU
    HAVE PEOPLE HURT YOU A LOT?

BUT IT'S PARADISE.
BUT IT'S PARADISE.
ALMOST PARADISE.
THAT I'VE MADE.

T-GIRL CHRISTIAN. If I learned anything from all this hell I went through is now I see the people. Used to be when I went into crowds or a party I would walk into a room and walk out the other end and no one ever knew I was in there. Now I walk in and it's, "Nancy Jo's here." Now I leave the dance floor and they shut it down. "Nancy's Jo's left, shut it down." Because I started seeing the people. The people who hurt, or the people who help. I'd never see that when I was trying to run from me. And this is a beautiful city. A lot of my friends say, "Well, why don't you just move, it's just too ornery, it's too hostile, they don't want you here." You know what, this is AMERICA, I like it here. I LIKE seeing Pikes Peak out of my front door. And I'll be doggoned if some guy is gonna to tell me where I can or can't live. The moment we have to run and hide and live in shadows, that is the moment when we have lost our liberties. And it's NOT gonna happen, not on my watch. You didn't get permission from me to be who you are, so damn sure I'm not gonna get permission from you to be who I am.

Scene 6

Free Yoself

Service at Emmanuel Baptist Church. Ben Reynolds' replacement is preaching.

NEW PASTOR AT EMMANUEL. God bless you. You may be seated. I'm ashamed a myself today, Emmanuel. Since taking over this pulpit a few weeks ago from Ben Reynolds, sometimes I find myself givin' in to weakness. Feeling tired. Wondering if God was going to be here to help me through this second sermon. After this morning's service, I let the Devil sneak up on me. And Miss Wanda said, "What happened to you? You had you a meltdown while we was gone?"

So I come with the question. God, is that you? Have you ever been in a situation and been at a point in time and wondered if you miss God talking to you, or working on you? How can you miss a God that's that big? God is so big that you can't confine him. Bigger than everything we can see. HOW can you miss some God that's this big? Amazing that sometime we don't recognize the answers to our prayers when God gives them to us.

But I say even Peter who walked with Jesus and prayed to God and was one of Jesus' disciples, even Peter when God spoke to him said "I don't know if this is live or if it's Memorex." I don't know if this thing is real. I don't know if this is God. I don't know if it's me. I don't know if it's a vision or if it's real. Maybe I shouldn't a eaten those pig feet last night and gone to bed." Is that you, God? Nobody sittin' next to you on the bus. Is that you, God? Nobody sittin' at the organ. Is that you God? Ask him. Now if you will remember, Peter finds himself in prison. Locked up and dealing with angels showing up and moving things and he makes the statement that "I wasn't sure if it was God or if I was dreaming." Well, lemme help you. One way to recognize when God is at work is that God always frees us from something. Because Peter was in prison and the scripture says he was being guarded, four units of guards. Sixteen guards. But they didn't understand something. You may lock me up but you can't lock God out. God has a way of finding me and coming to where I am! Anybody in here ever felt despair in the middle of the night, and all of a sudden God found you and all your troubles just disappeared? Anybody in here ever been driving down the street in your car, all by yourself, and you stuck in traffic, and some kinda way God knew your plate number, found your car, entered in your car and blessed you where you was? ANYBODY IN HERE EVER BEEN IN THE PRESENCE OF GOD! You may lock me up, but you can't lock God outta my life! The text says Peter was locked in the prison. The angel came in and started the freeing process. Ya'll gotta understand something, when God frees us, he takes us through a process. The angel walked in and the first thing the angel did was he walked up to Peter and touched him in his side. Get ready for the journey. Get up! Now, if some of you was Peter, you'd say wait, you want me to get up and dress myself? I got chains on my arms! But the scripture says when the angels gave Peter directions and Peter listened and got up and started to move, THE CHAINS FELL OFF! If you expect somebody to help you get outta your situation, you got to get up and get moving. When you wake up, get moving. Want to get a new job? Get up and put in an application. Looking for a mate to come to your house? Do yo' hair! Dress yo'self! Put on some nice clothes! Lose some weight! Wash your face! Put on some makeup! Put on your best suit! Put on a tie! And get movin'! It's a process and the process is: you can't be 'sleep in yo' prison!

Now, who the Son has set free is free indeed. So stop looking at other folk to validate you. Stop it. If your phone don't ring, CALL YO'SELF! STOP IT! If don't nobody lay hands on you, put your hands on your own head. BLESS YO'SELF! STOP IT! GOD is your validator. Stop waiting for the morning edition of the paper to come out to see if you made it through the night. Stop waiting for the morning edition of the paper to come out to see if you made it through the night.

Scene 7

Plan B

Song: Another Email From Ted.

SINGER.
    FROM TEDHAGGARD@GMAIL.COM
    DEAR FRIENDS:
    THANK YOU SO MUCH FOR WRITING.
    JESUS IS STARTING TO PUT ME BACK TOGETHER.
    HE AND HIS FOLLOWERS HAVE SAVED MY LIFE.
    THEY SENT GAYLE AND ME TO PHOENIX FOR A THREE-WEEK
        PSYCHOLOGICAL INTENSIVE
    THREE WEEKS THAT GAVE ME THREE YEARS' WORTH OF
        TREATMENT.
    GAYLE AND I HAVE DECIDED TO MOVE FROM COLORADO
        SPRINGS TO GO BACK TO SCHOOL.
    WE LOVE COLORADO SPRINGS SO MUCH,
    AND WILL ALWAYS REGARD THE BELIEVERS AT NEW LIFE
        CHURCH AS FAMILY,
    BUT WE HAVE TO GO.
(RHOP leader is driving. He appears projected as a video podcast.)
RHOP LEADER. All right … well, I told you all I'd do a video podcast as I'm driving to Kansas City and here I am. Driving. Nothing but snow. White tundra. Is tundra the right word? Is a tundra a place where snow is? Or is a tundra more of a desert … or a jungle … I don't know.
TED HAGGARD.
    WE HAVEN'T DECIDED WHERE WE ARE MOVING BUT SO FAR
        HAVE BEEN OFFERED TWO PLACES,
    ONE IN IOWA
    AND ONE IN MISSOURI.

WHERE WE PLAN TO GET ONLINE DEGREES IN PSYCHOLOGY
SO WE CAN SERVE OTHERS THE REST OF OUR LIVES.

RHOP LEADER. So my family and I are leaving the Springs, we're making a move, we need to get out to Kansas City, and maybe someone out there, God would lay it on their heart to pay our moving expenses. We've carried this baby of-of-of city transformation in Manitou Springs for a very long time. That was Plan A. I'll tell ya what — I believe possibly, now I don't know for sure, but I believe POSSIBLY that Plan A failed. Possibly. Plan A was for us to see revival happen to the people in this city. I believe that was Plan A. I think Plan B is now that we have to leave and go find the people. I think Plan B's OK. God help me. Kansas City, here I come.

TED HAGGARD.

    THANK YOU SO MUCH FOR YOUR LOVE AND PRAYERS DUR-
       ING THIS HORRIFIC TIME OF TRANSITION.

    FOR THE LAST THREE MONTHS, I'VE BEEN PARALYZED BY
       SHAME.

    BUT AS GOD AND PEOPLE LIKE YOU FORGIVE ME, THE SUN IS
       STARTING TO RISE IN MY LIFE,

    I LOOK FORWARD TO COMMUNICATING WITH GREATER EASE.

    GOD BLESS,

    TED HAGGARD

    "WE ARE EASTER PEOPLE."

ECONOMIC DEVELOPMENT WOMAN. There was an article recently in the paper, *The Gazette* here. It was called "Haggard's Vision Waning." And it's saying Ted's gone, Dobson's getting old, the evangelical movement is waning in Colorado Springs, political conservatives have lost. But I'm not so sure. Twenty-two years ago Ted Haggard had a vision that Colorado Springs would be an evangelical capitol. And twenty-two years ago, I was hired. I didn't know about Ted's vision. No. Never met him. But God used me to bring about that vision. And Colorado Springs became the evangelical capitol. *(Question.)* Yes I am comfortable with that. I know it's right. We're supposed to be here. And as Christians because we have the Bible, we know how the story ends. We win. *(Song: Pikes Peak [A Model Of Christian Charity].)*

    THEY SET OUT ON A SHIP CALLED THE *ARABELLA*
    FLEEING AN ENGLAND BOUND FOR HELL
    AND A CITY THEY BUILT ON A HILL TO DISPEL
    ALL THE EVIL IN THE WORLD
    AND FROM THAT WILDERNESS OF MASSACHUSETTS BAY
    THEY WOULD FORGE A NATION TO SHOW THE WAY

AMERICA WOULD SHINE ABOVE
A MODEL OF CHRISTIAN LOVE

BUT NO EDEN GREW IN THEIR NEW CANAAN
AND THEY WAITED FOR GOD THROUGH SNOW AND RAIN
IN THEIR EMPTY HOUSES WITH EMPTY SHELVES
AND THE WILDERNESS THEY DISCOVERED IN THEMSELVES.

THEY SAY THERE ARE NO SECOND ACTS IN AMERICAN LIVES
JUST SECOND MORTGAGES AND SECOND WIVES
AND WHEN THAT VISION JUST COULDN'T BE
AND THEY HAD NO PLAN B
THEY WERE LOST WITH NO WAY DOWN
FROM THAT CITY ON A HILL

THEY TRAVELLED WEST TO PIKES PEAK SUMMIT
TO A WILDERNESS UNTOUCHED THEY'D COME
IT WAS LIKE LOOKING AT HEAVEN THE VIEWS THAT PLUMMET
TEN THOUSAND FEET BELOW

AND THEY WOULD BUILD A CITY IN ALL THIS BEAUTY
AND GOD WOULD SHOW THE NATION ITS DUTY
FROM SUCH A DISTANT HEIGHT
THIS COUNTRY LOOKED ALL RIGHT

BUT WHEN I HIKE TO THE TOP OF PIKES PEAK NOW
OR IF I DRIVE MY CAR UP, IT JUST TAKES AN HOUR
THERE'S A DONUT SHOP, AND A PARKING LOT
THE PEOPLE JUST LOOK SMALL
IT'S JUST A PHOTO OP AFTER ALL

AND IF THERE WAS A BACKUP PLAN FOR AMERICAN FOLK
NOT JUST SECOND AMENDMENTS AND SECONDHAND SMOKE
COULD WE LEAVE THE VISION ON THE MOUNTAINTOP
WITH THE FROSTBITE AND THE SNOW
DO WE EVEN KNOW WHICH WAY TO GO
TO LIVE TOGETHER IN THE CITY BELOW

I JUST DON'T KNOW, YOU KNOW

I JUST DON'T KNOW
I JUST DON'T KNOW, YOU KNOW
I JUST DON'T KNOW
GROUP 1.
    I JUST DON'T KNOW, YOU KNOW
    I JUST DON'T KNOW
    I JUST DON'T KNOW, YOU KNOW
    I JUST DON'T KNOW

GROUP 2.
    IT'S A LONG ROAD TO COLORADO
    IT'S A LONG ROAD TO COLORADO

GROUP 3.
    WHERE ARE WE GOING
    HOW DO WE GET THERE
    WHAT IS YOUR PLAN FOR THIS THIS THIS BEAUTIFUL CITY
    WHERE ARE WE GOING
    HOW DO WE GET THERE
    WHAT IS YOUR PLAN FOR THIS THIS THIS BEAUTIFUL CITY
TRAILS GUIDE #4. For a safe trip to the Rockies, heed these final words of advice. No guide, no map can guarantee you won't get lost. But suppose it happens. Do not panic. Virtually all people who get lost are eventually found, either alive or dead, so the idea is to stay alive no matter how long you have to stay lost. So good luck.

End of Play

PROPERTY LIST

Trails Guide
Newspaper
Coffee mugs
Clipboards
Referendum I flyers
Balloons

SOUND EFFECTS

Doorbells
Online sounds
Election cheering